MY FAVOURITE CHRISTMAS TREE

SANTA WITH OUR GIFTS

SANTA ON THE SLEDGE

REINDEER HERE FOR CHRISTMAS

SANTA IS NEXT DOOR

GINGERBREAD MAN

HOUSE WITH CHRISTMAS DECORATION

SNOW GLOBE

CHRISTMAS GIFTS FRESH FROM SANTA

CHRISTMAS ELF

CHRISTMAS TREE

CHRISTMAS BELLS

CHRISTMAS ANGEL

CHRISTMAS STAR

CHIMNEY FOR SANTA

CHRISTMAS COOKIES

HOT CHOCOLATE FEELS JUST RIGHT

SNOWBALLING ON CHRISTMAS

POLA BEAR

IGLOO

FROSTY SNOWMAN'S HAT

SNOW ANGEL

CHRISTMAS BOW

POINSETTIA FLOWERS

SNOWY OWL

CANDY SHOP

CHRISTMAS BOWS

SNOWY STREETS

TEDDY BEAR ON SANTA HAT

FESTIVE GARLAND

NUTCRACKER SOLDIER

JOLLY SNOWMAN FACE

CHRISTMAS MORNING

TOY WORKSHOP

CHRISTMAS MARKET

ANGIE AND FRIENDS SINGING CAROLS

SNOWY HILLS

HORSES SINGING CAROLS

NORTHPOLE MAILBOX

SNOWY FOREST

CHRISTMAS PARTY

CANDY STREET

TWINKLING STARS AND MOON

CHRISTMAS FEAST

FAMILY ON CHRISTMAS PYJAMAS

SNOW ANIMALS

SANTA'S WORKSHOP

MAILBOX TO POST CHRISTMAS WISHES

CHRISTMAS BAKING

SNOW VILLAGE

TOY TRAIN

CHRISTMAS MOON

CAROLING SNOWMEN

CHILDREN GOING FOR CAROL

SANTA PREPARING OUR GIFTS

CHRISTMAS AND GIFT SHARING

SANTA READING THE WISH LISTS

OUR SLEDGE OF GIFTS

CHRISTMAS DUCK

CHRISTMAS ORNAMENTS

CHRISTMAS ANGEL WITH TRUMPET

SNOWMAN

CHRISTMAS ORNAMENTS

HOLLY BERRIES

MARY , JOSEPH, JESUS , 3 WISE MEN

WINTER HAT

ICE SKATES

CHRISTMAS SOCKS

POLAR BEARS SINGING CAROL

JACK IN BOOTS

CHURCH

HAPPY SNOWMAN

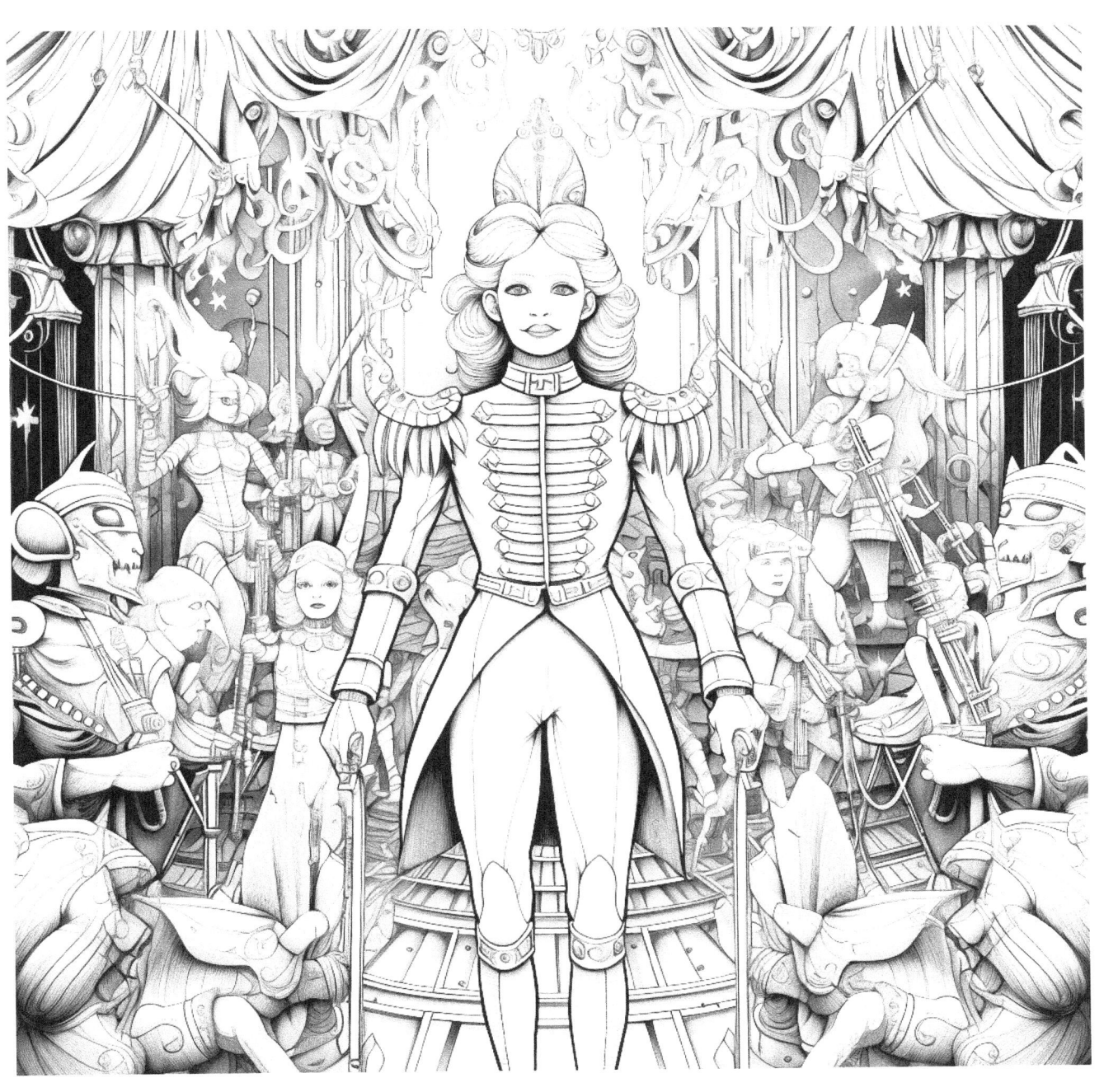

NUTCRACKER BALLET

TINSEL

CHRISTMAS CRAFTS

KIDS , DOG ON A SLEDGE

CHRISTMAS PARADE

CHRISTMAS TREE FARM

SAM THE SNOW MAN

ADDORNED CHRISTMAS TREE

CHRISTMAS GLOBE

CHRISTMAS SLEDGE

SANTA WITH MANY PRESENTS

SANTA TAKING HOT CHOCOLATE

TOM OPENING THE GIFT BOXES

GINGERBREAD MAN WITH CANDY

NUTCRACKER

CHRISTMAS GIFTBOX

CHRISTMAS TEDDY

CHRISTMAS FIREPLACE

OUR CHRISTMAS WISHES

CHRISTMAS ANGEL WITH TRUMPET

CHRISTMAS DUCK WITH CANDY CANE

SANTA IS ON THE WAY

SAM IS ON THE SLEDGE

WELCOME SANTA

TIMMY IS HAPPY

Meowy Christmas